MW00413315

Lefties

Lefties

A BOOK FOR SOUTHPAWS

Margaret Lannamann

Illustrated by **Joe Stites**

AriEL BooKS

Andrews McMeel Publishing

Kansas City

Lefties:
A Book for Southpaws

ISBN: 0-7407-0512-1
Library of Congress Catalog Card Number:
99-65536

*The
left hand
is the
hand
of the
heart.*
—Old
Italian
proverb

Introduction

Left-handers struggle daily to cope in a right-handed world, but they have much to be proud of. Studies suggest that lefties tend to be more imaginative, artistic, musical, and athletic than their right-handed comrades. Luminaries such as Albert Einstein, Michelangelo, Babe Ruth, Marilyn Monroe, and Bob Dylan are a few of the many left-handers who have made their mark on history.

Right-handers, who are governed by the left side of the brain, tend to be practical,

Lefties

organized, and reasonable—
some might even say a bit boring. Left-handers, who are
governed by the right side of
the brain, are not so down-to-
earth. Instead, they are apt to
be original, humorous, impul-
sive, creative, perhaps even a
little exasperating—but never,
never boring.

So the next time you're trying unsuccessfully to use a pair of scissors, write in a spiral binder, or play with a

Lefties

deck of cards, take a deep
breath, straighten your
shoulders, and smile. Don't let
the frustrations of can openers
and keyboards get you down.
Be proud of being a southpaw.

Left-
handed-
ness is
cause for
celebration!

15

Anthropologists believe that humans showed a preference for right- and left-handedness as far back as 1.4 million years ago.

About one out of every ten people is left-handed.

Lefties

Left-hander Jim Henson,
creator of the Muppets,
exhibited characteristics
that are typical of left-handed
people: enormous creativity,
whimsical humor, and a
certain endearing quirkiness.
Kermit the Frog even plays
his banjo left-handed.

Some experts believe that more than one-third of all children would be left-handed if they weren't encouraged in any way to be right-handed—which is unlikely to happen, given that the world we live in is set up for righties.

The term "southpaw" was coined by Chicago sportswriter Charles Seymour in the 1890s to describe left-handed pitchers, who, due to the way some old ballparks were situated, threw with their arms facing south.

Lefties

Certain animals tend toward left-handedness, especially lemurs and parrots.

21

M. C. Escher used to say that his left-handedness helped his ability to draw the intricate, illogical, inside-out drawings for which he is famous.

"I may be left-handed, but I'm always right."

—ANONYMOUS

Lefties

Left-hander Jimi Hendrix couldn't afford to pay for a more expensive left-handed guitar when he was learning to play, so he used a right-handed guitar—upside down!

Many experts believe that forcing a naturally left-handed child to become right-handed

Lefties

can result in stuttering, read-
ing problems, difficulty in
telling left from right, and
general feelings of inadequacy.

25

Although 10 percent of the general population is left-handed, 14 percent of all professional baseball players are left-handed, and 26 percent of baseball pitchers are left-handed.

There is a town in West
Virginia called Left Hand.
Many of the people who live
there may be right-handed,
but each of them is at the
same time a Left Hander!

27

Early printers had to set type by hand, and therefore needed to be able to read and write backward. Not surprisingly, left-handers such as Benjamin Franklin gravitated toward this vocation.

Lefties

Left-hander Napoléon
Bonaparte, well known in
school for his illegible hand-

writing and inability to spell
correctly, became a brilliant
military tactician who went on
to conquer much of Europe.

A left-handed compliment
is one that has a sarcastic
undertone that is not
complimentary at all.

Lefties

Bart Simpson and his creator, Matt Groening, are both left-handed.

Tip: If you are trying to fish with a right-handed rod,

try turning the reel upside
down and reeling backward.

The world of *Alice in Wonder-
land,* and especially *Through
the Looking-Glass,* is very
"left-handed"—everything is
the wrong way around and
inside out. But then, Lewis
Carroll was left-handed.

Lefties

Left-handed baseball players are legion: Casey Stengel, Babe Ruth, Reggie Jackson, Yogi Berra, Lou Gehrig, Ty Cobb, Sandy Koufax, Don Mattingly—and then there was Mickey Mantle, who was a prolific switch-hitter.

33

Of the twelve astronauts who have walked on the moon, four are left-handed.

35

Left-handed people, especially if forced to use the right hand as children, often confuse clockwise and counterclockwise. Some use a jingle to help them remember: "righty tighty, lefty loosey."

Lefties

Surprisingly, some identical twins, who have exactly the same genes, may not both be lefties or righties.

37

If you carry a rabbit's foot for good luck, the left hind foot is supposed to be the most potent.

Some things in today's world actually give lefties an advantage, such as ATMs, fast-food

Lefties

windows, tollbooths, and participation in certain sports, baseball in particular.

39

Michelangelo's statue *David* shows David holding his sling in his left hand. Also, in the artist's paintings on the ceiling of the Sistine Chapel, God is stretching out his left hand to Adam. It should

Lefties

come as no surprise that
Michelangelo was left-handed!

Tip: A computer mouse
designed for a
right-hander
can some-
times be con-
verted for use
by a left-hander

by going into the control
panel and making certain
adjustments.

*The number of left-handed
movie stars* is surprisingly
large, and includes such giants
as Robert Redford, Greta
Garbo, Tom Cruise, Emma
Thompson, Peter Fonda, Cary

Lefties

Grant, Kim Novak, Bruce
Willis, Nicole Kidman, Marilyn
Monroe, Matt Dillon, and Julia
Roberts.

Alexander the Great, the
renowned conqueror and
visionary, is one of the earliest
left-handers documented in
history.

43

Merry-go-rounds are right-handed: Riders have to reach for the brass ring with their right hand.

A pregnant forty-year-old woman is more likely to give birth to a left-handed baby than a pregnant twenty-five-year-old woman.

45

"Left-handed people tend to be more creative, more imaginative than right-handed people."

—Dr. Brying Bryngelson

Left-handed tennis players excel at their sport. Consider Jimmy Connors, John McEnroe, Monica Seles, and Martina Navratilova.

The
reason why
very few jet
pilots are left-handed is
because the control panel is
placed in the center of the
cockpit where a right-hander
sitting in the left-hand seat

(the captain's seat) can reach it easily. A lefty, however, has to lean over awkwardly to reach the controls.

Things that are difficult for lefties to use include scissors,

Lefties

watches, thermometers, play-
ing cards, some sports equip-
ment, a mouse for a computer,
phone booths, drinking foun-
tains, spiral notebooks, loose-
leaf binders, corkscrews, can
openers, slot machines at casi-
nos, cameras and camcorders,
soup ladles, power saws,
pocket knives, file cabinets

with latches, pens chained in
banks, pencil sharpeners, and
ice-cream scoops.

The trait of left-handedness
is related to musical talent
because pitch perception and
sense of rhythm are centered
in the right side of the brain.
Cole Porter, Bob Dylan, Paul

McCartney, Jimi Hendrix, Crystal Gale, Sergei Rachmaninoff, Rudy Valee, Paul Simon, Phil Collins, and Melissa Manchester are a few examples of the many talented musicians who are left-handed.

51

Anthropologists have reason
to believe that one-third of the
Native American population
was left-handed at one time.

Lefties

In the early 1990s, two
Canadian psychologists pro-
moted the idea that left-
handers have shorter life spans
than right-handers. They theo-
rized that because lefties use
machines and appliances
designed for righties, they are
more prone to accidental
death. Fortunately, this

theory
has been
completely
disproved.

Children whose parents are
both right-handed have a 10
percent chance of being left-
handed. Children whose parents are both left-handed have

Lefties

more than a 40 percent
chance of being left-handed.

*The number
of* talented
left-handed
comedians
is high,
and
includes

such stars as Harpo Marx, Richard Pryor, Don Rickles, Dick Van Dyke, Carol Burnett, Jay Leno, Charlie Chaplin, Danny Kaye, and Jerry Seinfeld.

Certain notorious criminals have been left-handed, notably Billy the Kid, the

Boston Strangler, John Dillinger, and Jack the Ripper.

"If the right side of the body is controlled by the left side of the brain, and the left side of the body is controlled by the

right side of the brain, then
left-handed people are the only
ones in their right minds."

—ANONYMOUS

*Golf may be the most
difficult sport* for a left-hander
to play. In fact, some lefties
teach themselves to play right-
handed to avoid the perceived

Lefties

disadvantage of being left-handed. In recent years, however, left-handed golf has been gaining wider acceptance, and left-handed clubs are available at most sporting goods stores.

59

The percentage of left-handers that makes up the high-IQ society Mensa is 20 percent, or double what you would expect, since only 10 percent of the population is left-handed.

Tip: If you, like many left-handers, have trouble figuring your right from your left, try

this: Hold out your hands, and
the one that makes an "L"
with the forefinger and thumb
is the left hand.

61

Pablo Picasso, viewed by many as the greatest and most influential artist of the twentieth century, was left-handed.

Some studies suggest that left-handers have a harder

Lefties

time
falling
asleep
than
right-
handers.

In England, South Africa,
Japan, Australia, Zimbabwe,
and a number of other coun-

63

tries, cars are driven on
the left side of the road. In
England, the custom started
in the Middle Ages so that a
traveler's right hand,
or sword hand,
was available
to fight off
passing
outlaws.

Lefties

**"*Right-handers* are a bunch
of chocolate soldiers. If you've
seen one, you've seen 'em all.
But left-handers are some-
thing else again."**

—Dr. Joseph Bogan

Statistics show that females
are less likely to be left-handed
than males. In fact, for every

65

100 left-handed females, there are 150 left-handed males.

One out of six presidents of the United States has been left-handed: James Garfield, Herbert Hoover,

Lefties

Harry S. Truman, Gerald Ford, Ronald Reagan, George Bush, and Bill Clinton.

A left-handed baseball player has some definite advantages over a right-handed player:

When pitching, he can watch a runner at first base more easily than a righty, and a lefty batter, who is facing first base at the completion of his swing, is one step closer to first base when he begins his run.

Tip: When writing in a spiral notebook or a three-ring

Lefties

binder, start at the back and
write on the other side of the
page. It helps to tilt the paper
to the right, not the left—this
makes it easier to write for
long periods
without hav-
ing your
hand
cramp.

69

Spiral notebooks that are bound at the top work well.

In ancient Japan, a man could divorce his wife if he learned that she was left-handed. Even now, left-handedness is so frowned upon in Japan that only 2 percent of the population is openly left-handed.

Lefties

George Bush, Bill Clinton, and Ross Perot, the three major contenders in the 1992 United States presidential election, were all left-handed.

The Boy Scout handshake is always made with the left hand because it is nearer the heart.

Lefties

Many baseball, football,
and soccer players believe it is
good luck to put their left
socks and shoes on first.

The great left-handed painter
Leonardo da Vinci filled many
notebooks with his writings,
which were written in a tiny,
backward, mirror script that

73

went
across
the
page
from
right to left.

Marcel Marceau, who many
believe is the world's greatest
mime, is left-handed.

Lefties

Many left-handed movie stars
exhibit a delightful kookiness,
such as Shirley MacLaine,
Judy Garland, Diane Keaton,
Robert De Niro, Whoopi
Goldberg, and Goldie Hawn.

The left-handed composer
Sergei Rachmaninoff had
the widest hand span ever

Lefties

measured on a pianist:
His left hand could span
twelve white keys, or
one-and-a-half octaves.

*International Left-Handers
Day* was celebrated on August
13, 1976, for the first time.

77

Web sites for left-handers:

Left Hand Publishing:

Information, publications, surveys, and sources of products for left-handers.

www.lefthandpublishing.com

Gauche! Left-Handers in Society: Information and coping strategies for left-handers

Lefties

living in a right-handed world.

www.indiana.edu/~primate/lspeak9.html

Lefty's Top Ten: List of top ten annoyances, stores selling left-handed books and products, and organizations for left-handers.

www.members.home.net/
computer-goddess/lefties/

Rosemary West's Left-Handed Page: A number of links to other sites related to  left-handedness, including humor, music, articles, shopping, sports, and more.

www.rosemarywest.com/left/

Designed by **BTD**NYC

*Set in Clearface, Variex, and
Triplex by* **BTD**NYC

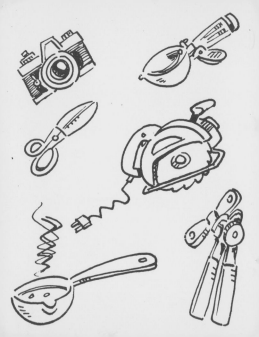